Praise for "Winning"

"I started receiving *The Weekend Briefing* just as I transitioned into fundraising. Rob was my first mentor and he didn't even know it. 'Winning' truly incorporates all that is great about Rob's approach to fundraising. Practice the Five Truths and the donor will win, your organization will win and you, the gift officer, will win."

Allison Nickle Egidi
Associate Vice President for Development
University of Virginia

"Rob Cummings' 'Winning' boils our work in philanthropy down to its essential elements. Our profession, at its best, is still about spending time in the right way; developing relationships, listening, and saying thank you really well. Rob understands this and, through stories, brings to life the lessons that will help development officers at any stage of their career."

Jonathan E. Bridge
Assistant Head of School for Advancement
University School
Hunting Valley, OH

"As fundraisers, I view us as storytellers and you are a masterful storyteller. That comes through time and again in this book. This book is a must-read for any fundraising professional– whether just starting in the field or seasoned veteran. All nonprofit professionals can learn from this book. Most importantly, Rob gets to the heart of reminding us why we do this noble work."

Joel Cencius, CFRE
Vice President of Development
Big Brothers Big Sisters of
Metro Milwaukee

Winning

The Five Truths of Fundraising

Rob Cummings

First paperback edition, November 2019

ISBN-13: 978-1-7342524-1-5 (paperback)
ISBN-13: 978-1-7342524-0-8 (ebook)

Library of Congress Control Number: 2019917994

Written in Lemont, Illinois, United States

Photo of Rob Cummings by Emily Cummings

https://theweekendbriefing.com

A gift from the net proceeds of this book will be made to Sojourner Truth House, serving homeless and at-risk women and their children in Gary, Indiana.

To learn more about this wonderful place, visit: https://www.sojournertruthhouse.org/.

Table of Contents

Foreword

"Rob, there's a book in there somewhere."

In 11 years of writing the *Weekend Briefing* I heard that gentle nudge from many of my heroes in our profession.

So I set out to find that book. It took a while, but I did. "Winning" brings together the best of the *Weekend Briefing* with the most important fundraising lessons I've learned in the last four decades.

Over coffee one morning a friend told me, "I don't know how you manage to write the Briefing every Sunday night, year after year. It must be a labor of love."

He's right. And so is this book.

"We are in the twilight of a society based on data.

"As information and intelligence become the domain of computers, society will place more value on the one human ability that cannot be automated: emotion.

"Imagination, myth, ritual – the language of emotion – will affect everything, from our purchasing decisions to how we work with others.

"Organizations will thrive on the basis of their stories and myths.

"Organizations will need to understand that their products are less important than their stories."

ROLF JENSEN, COPENHAGEN INSTITUTE
FOR FUTURE STUDIES

ADAPTED FROM "STORYTELLING AS BEST
PRACTICE" FOURTH EDITION,
BY ANDY GOODMAN

The Five Truths

Hanging on the wall in our study is one of my favorite pieces of art. In a carved wooden frame sits a piece of parchment with a saying written in four-color uncial calligraphy. It reminds me of a page from a medieval manuscript.

The saying reads:

> *Dance as if no one is watching,*
> *Sing as if no one is listening, and*
> *Live every day as if it were your last.*

Do you think about that sometimes? I'm thinking about it now. What if this was the last Briefing? What would be the final thought I'd want to share with you?

I would want you to know how you can compete. And how you can win.

There are five truths you need to embrace. Only five. Long ago I scribbled them down and earlier today I went back and looked at that scrap of paper. Only five? Yes. This is really it? Yes. The five things you need to know, cling to, and live every day of your professional life.

One. You need to believe. In yourself and your ability. In your organization, and in the important work it does. When you shake the donor's hand, the look in your eye needs to radiate quiet

1

confidence in the invitation you are about to extend. There is no apologizing ("I'm so sorry to bother you! I know how busy you are!"), and nothing to suggest you are a bother. You stand tall, with a smile, with pride and enthusiasm. You are there to assist that person in the great things she or he wants to do. Never waver in your belief.

Two. You will not win by sitting behind your desk. Get out. Make visits. Over time, you'll see the number of visits increase and the purpose of the visits moving from introduction to cultivation to asking to closing. It is very difficult to ask for a gift before you've established a relationship with that person. Take the time to do that. Don't make visits willy-nilly. Use data and anecdotal information to determine the 40, 100, and 200 most important donors and/or potential donors for your organization. Forty, because that's how many true relationships you'll be able to manage. One hundred, because that's the rough number of a major gift officer's prospect pool. And 200, because that's the number of potential donors you need to identify to have five visits a week, the gold standard.

Three. Put the donor first. It is not about you. Think of the donors' dreams to make a difference, not what you want to "get out of them." Think of what they want to know and why they should care about your request. "Impact investing" is just a trendy way of expressing the time-worn notion that we need to tell donors what their gift will accomplish. Seek to understand, not to be understood.

Four. Be better than any other organization in saying "thank you." Smaller shops have a decided advantage in this because they have the capacity to make a $1,000 donor feel really appreciated. Constantly work at being the best at saying thank you, and not only at the moment a gift is made. Learning how to be great at saying thank you is more important than learning how to be great at asking for a gift.

Five. Focus on the right things. There are a million distractions in your day. Don't let them beat you. A million ways you can spend your time: webinars, requests from faculty, a pitch from a vendor. One of the most important pieces of advice I ever received was "Don't be such a nice guy." Every one of my heroes in our profession has the ability to focus on the single most important thing at the moment with a look in their eye that shouts their determination to get the job done. And they're still nice!

That's it. Truly. Oh, I suppose you could tack on another thought or two, things that speak to the unrealistic expectations disheartening too many fundraisers and sinking too many shops. But if you decide that you want to win and think about these five truths every day, you will win.

The beauty for all of us is that we don't have to beat the other guy in order to succeed. There's room for all of us to win.

These Five Truths will get you there.

Some time ago I was at a conference and got to know a talented young development professional.

During the break from a morning session he turned to me and said, "You know Rob, the very best thing about development is that everybody wins.

"The student, or whomever is the ultimate beneficiary of the gift, that person wins.

"The donor wins.

"The institution wins.

"And the development officer wins.

"I love that about our work."

I told him, and I will tell you, those are profound words.

The First Truth:

Belief

No one is going to believe in you until you believe in yourself.

Bobby

It was time for lunch. I got up from my desk and headed for the little kitchen in our office suite. I was the Alumni Director.

The president and the VP for development were standing in the hallway locked in earnest conversation. They both looked frazzled.

"What are you guys talking about?" I asked.

The VP answered.

"Joe keeps promising a scholarship. We've tried everything we can think of, but he keeps dodging us."

The president nodded and gave me a look that said, "If you have any bright ideas, I'm all ears."

I did.

"I'd like a shot. Let me try to get that gift."

What made me say that? Was it competition with the VP? The challenge of it? A hunch? Whatever it was, I'd thrown down the gauntlet and Tim, the VP, was not pleased.

He stifled a snort, rolled his eyes and gave the president a look as if to say, "You've got to be kidding." But instead, the president looked me square in the eye and said, "Okay, but I want cash on the barrel-head."

I grinned, forgot about lunch, and headed for the phone.

Walking into Joe's auto dealership I was mindful of the old saying, "Be careful what you wish for, you might just get it." I imagined Tim's look if I came back empty-handed.

Could I "seize the moment?"

I was ready to find out.

Joe was busy selling a nice young couple a car. I cooled my heels for 15 minutes pretending to be interested in the Buicks. I could hear Joe's booming voice and see handshakes in the doorway. My chance was getting close.

"Come on in! Great to see ya!"

The walls in Joe's office were covered with photos of him with quite possibly every celebrity in town. Even before I sat down Joe pressed his lucky charm, a tiny horseshoe, into my palm while looking very pleased with himself. I tried a few icebreakers to establish some kind of connection. I would send along my mother-in-law's recipe for chicken cacciatore. As if he cared.

Then I got down to business. "Joe, I know you and Father have been talking and I want to thank you for considering a gift of a scholarship."

Click. I could immediately see him switch off, thinking "How fast can I get this guy out of my office?" I had to say the right thing and say it fast.

"Joe, let me tell you about the student who would receive your scholarship." And I just kept going.

"Bobby and his brother both attend school on full scholarships. To help work off his scholarship, Bobby sweeps the halls after school every day with one of those big double-handled push brooms."

Joe was listening.

"Yesterday, Bobby was pushing his broom down the hall and our president was walking toward him. When they passed each other Bobby stopped, stuck out his hand and shook the president's hand.

"Father was a little surprised and asked, 'Bobby, I'm always glad to shake your hand, but why today?'"

Joe was listening as if nothing else in the world mattered at that moment.

"Bobby told him, 'Father, I just found out at lunch today that my scholarship was renewed for next year.

"'I guess I just had to say thank you to somebody.'

"Joe, I hope you'll be the guy to give this kid a scholarship."

And then I shut up.

Joe was staring at me. He put his cigar down in the ash tray. "How much is a scholarship?" I told him.

"I'm leaving for Europe in ten days. Before I go, you'll have your money."

I stood up and shook his hand.

Eight days later, the check came. Within two years, after enough time had passed for me to develop a true relationship between Joe and the school, he gave $150,000 to the campaign. Two years later, $350,000 to renovate the gym.

Two years after that, Joe pledged a mid-seven figure gift to his University. I guess they were paying attention.

I never forgot the lesson Joe taught me. People don't want to support the annual fund. That means nothing to them. They want to make a difference to someone like Bobby. We just need the quiet confidence to tell the story, and ask.

And Tim? He taught me that no one is going to believe in you until you believe in yourself.

What Donors Are Starving For

The ballroom was packed. The chairman stepped up to the podium, took a look around and said, "Rather than speak to you tonight, I want you to hear these words that inspire me every day."

The lights dimmed. The crowd murmured. Faintly, then louder and louder were the sounds of an orchestra and Frank Sinatra singing. On two giant screens to accompany the song were photos of teachers working with students, coaches and their teams, alumni meeting their scholarship recipients, and volunteers at the Phonathon.

The song Sinatra was singing? "Here's to the Winners." It lasted two and a half minutes. There was not a dry eye in the house. The entire room jumped to their feet and cheered.

There was nothing left to be said. "Here's to the winners all of us can be."

The phone rang. Phil was calling. He got right to the point. "So how's it going?"

"Phil," I told him, "it's going great!"

"You son of a gun," he said in mild exasperation, "Every time I call, you tell me the exact same thing – it's going great."

Somehow, I was inspired to answer,

"Phil, if I don't tell you things are great at your alma mater, who's going to?"

Silence. "You know what, my friend?" he said, "You're right."

That's what our donors want to hear. They want to hear it's going great. They want to jump to their feet and cheer. They want their association with our organizations to make them happy.

They don't want to hear about our problems. Or our struggles. They have plenty of their own. Donors want to hear about our successes, our victories, and how their gifts made them happen.

Every donor I know wants to be associated with a winner. The tricky part is that "being a winner" is something the donor perceives about us. It's not something we can "do," like making an ask or sending a letter.

What makes you a "winner" to your donor? I think it boils down to four things.

Look like a winner. Stand up straight. Smile when you say hello. Take pride in your personal appearance. Does your building shine? Is the lobby welcoming? Does your communication, down to every single thing the donor receives, reflect how you want to be perceived? None of this is expensive. It just takes a little care and effort. Being "classy" is not the same as "gaudy" or "expensive."

Think like your donors. They are desperate to feel appreciated. By anyone! Give it to them! Make your donors feel so genuinely appreciated that they want to be with you more than with your competition.

Share the success. Every single day, look for the good in your organization and find someone to share it with. Think of organizations you perceive as winners. Why do you think that way about them? It's because of good news or success you're heard from them recently. Your pride and enthusiasm in your organization is a "drug" to your donors and they want some of it!

And finally, live "quiet confidence." When I told Phil things were going great, it wasn't just what I said but how I said it. Every great fundraiser I know lives quiet confidence. Not cocky, not even close to that. A quiet confidence in themselves, in the message they have to share, in the organization they represent.

Here's to the winners all of us can be.

The Two Secrets

There are two secrets that separate the great fundraisers from the not-yet-great.

I should stop there for a second. Do you fall into the "not-yet-great" category? Do you want to be a great fundraiser? Then go ahead. Become one! Nobody's stopping you!

Well, that's not true, exactly. Your boss, or your board may be stopping you from becoming a great fundraiser. There is an epidemic in the nonprofit world of unrealistic expectations, as insidious as the Ebola virus, that is killing development shops and fundraisers alike. Killing their spirit, mostly. It's shameful.

Anyway, despite that, if you want to be a great fundraiser, I wish I could be there with you right now, put my two hands on your shoulders, look you right in the eye and tell you, "You can do this." You really can.

Great fundraisers come in all shapes and sizes, young and old and in between, men and women, chubby and skinny, fashionable and not-so-fashionable. Doesn't matter.

What matters is that you believe you can be great. That you want to be. You want to practice this wonderful craft of ours, this great study of human nature, giving people a chance to do something that will make them feel great about themselves and make a difference to a cause, to an organization that you are proud to serve.

Here are the two secrets. Well, one's not a secret so much as it's just the truth. Great fundraisers get that way because they engage in the process all the time. They know who their top 40 donors and prospects are and they care about them. Those donors and prospects know the fundraiser cares about them, so much so that the donor doesn't regard the person as a fundraiser but as a friend.

The great fundraiser, because she or he does this all the time, knows how to create a relationship and how to nurture it. He or she is attuned to the moment of "the spark," the occasion when that relationship can begin, and the great fundraiser never lets that moment pass by unclaimed. But again, she knows how to do this because she does it all the time! That's the first thing that makes a fundraiser great: engaging in the process, over and over again.

If you do, and if you care enough to pay attention to the times you flub up (and trust me, there will be many of those times), you will become more comfortable, more confident in the process of developing the relationship. You will know when the donor is ready for you to invite their investment in your organization, and how to work with the donor TO MEET THEIR NEEDS AS WELL AS YOURS in making the gift happen.

So, the first thing is, get your hands dirty. The great fundraisers have been working in their own gardens getting their hands dirty for years.

The second thing that separates the great fundraisers from the not-yet-great is a trade secret. I'm going to share it with you right now.

In the beginning, in the earliest stages of forming the relationship with the prospective donor that you hope and trust will lead to a major gift, the donor is not thinking about making a gift, or what the gift will support, or even your organization itself. Your donor is thinking of none of those things.

Your prospective donor is sizing you up. He or she, or they, are deciding if they want to work with you. If they like you. If you are worth their time and attention. There is a moment along the way (it is different every time) when the donor reaches their tipping point with you and decides you are worth their trust. It is at that moment when they will start to pay attention to the gift opportunity you want to discuss with them.

The secret to bringing your donor to her or his tipping point with you? Simple. Be yourself. Be the good, honorable, honest person you are. Think about how you'd like a fundraiser to relate to you if the tables were turned. Are you cocky? Pushy? Phony? If so, that tipping point is a long way away.

But if you're yourself, just yourself, representing your organization with pride, wearing that enthusiasm on your sleeve, listening to the donor and paying attention, you become the person the donor wants to enter into a relationship with. You'll know the tipping point because you care enough about what you do to get out there and be a major gift officer, not just dream about it.

As the late Steve Jobs said, "Your time in this world is limited, so don't waste it living someone else's life. Don't be trapped by dogma, which is living with the results of other people's thinking. Don't let the noise of others' opinions drown out your own inner voice.

"Have the courage to follow your heart and intuition. They somehow know what you truly want to become."

At the end of the day, believing in yourself is about not being afraid.

Are you afraid? Even a little bit? You're not alone. Most fundraisers are, about some aspect of their work.

After the U.S. Women's soccer team won the World Cup, Abby Wambach was talking to the next generation of women soccer players and she told them, "You have the ability to be anything you want to be as long as you work hard and believe in yourself."

She was talking to fundraisers, too. You can be anything you want to be. You can be a great fundraiser. Honestly, you can. Do you want to be?

The only thing holding you back is being afraid.

Are you afraid to ask someone face-to-face for a gift? To finally get that big project done? To reach out to a donor you neglected? To admit what you don't know?

Are you afraid to reconnect with an old friend in development? To tell your boss your idea? To make four visits a week your number one priority?

Are you afraid to find out how good you really can be?

Being a great fundraiser is about having courage, if you want to know the truth. My gosh, if we have that courage, we have right in our hands the chance to make the kind of difference in the world other people dream about and never have the chance to do.

Don't be afraid. Never give up. Believe in yourself.

The Second Truth:

Make Visits

It's either a good visit, or a good story.

"Just Ask"

The school president met Harry, Class of '62, for lunch downtown. Harry was a successful commodities broker. He attended reunions and other events from time to time.

The president had called Harry out of the blue and asked for the visit. Harry, a loyal annual fund donor, said 'yes' right away.

When the salad came, the president asked Harry for a gift of $20,000 to fund scholarships at the school. Harry said he would be glad to do that. Business completed, the rest of the lunch was just a nice conversation.

Over dessert, the president put down his fork, looked at his lunch companion and said, "Harry, can I ask you a question? Don't get me wrong, I am grateful for this generous gift. But the largest contribution you've ever made to the school was $100.

"Why haven't you done anything like this before?"

Harry smiled. "Honestly? Because no one's ever asked me."

Everything we do in advancement centers around one thing: The Ask. All the alumni magazines and donor events, all our cultivation and stewardship have one thing, one moment, as their fulcrum.

It's that beautiful moment when fundraising and philanthropy connect. When the invitation is extended, and the invitation is accepted. The Ask.

The Five Truths of Fundraising

Without The Ask, nothing happens.

The late Barry Cicero was toastmaster of the alumni banquet for 26 years and an immense help to a neophyte alumni director. Barry's first love, though, was the American Legion. One day he gave me a pin they used to recruit new members. Just above the Legion logo were the words, "Just Ask."

When he gave it to me, Barry smiled and said, "That's what we have to do if we want to keep going. You too, I imagine."

I hold that pin in my hand every day.

People look at our world today from any angle and say, "What a mess. I only wish I could do something to make a difference."

We, you and I, are among the lucky few who actually CAN make a difference. If we choose to.

If we choose to Ask.

I was up in Minnesota for an event. George had invited me to play golf with him that morning at his club. I played lousy but we had fun and more important, we got to know each other. That night, as he and Anne were leaving the event, I walked them to the door.

"I know you both are really focused on the campaign at your church. But if you're able to help us toward the end of the year with a gift for scholarships, it would be so appreciated."

They stopped in their tracks. George looked at Anne and then at me.

"You know, we have a fund we haven't done anything with in a long time. The distributions have to be used for scholarships. This would be perfect."

Anne was nodding and smiling. George continued. "Yes, we can. We can do something significant for that." They never stopped smiling as I bade them good night.

When all the talking heads are gone, at the moment of truth, it's just you and the donor. You, with your sweaty palms, perhaps. But also, you with your courage. And with your belief in your cause. At that moment, there's nothing left but to Just Ask.

Only one thing is required. Conviction. Nerve. Moxie. Courage. Guts.

Call it what you will.

Do you have it? I think you do.

The Spark

I've heard this so many times, I could barf.

"We've gotta send a proposal to Oprah!" "We need to ask Bill Gates for a gift!"

No, you don't. Oprah and Bill Gates don't know you from a hill of beans. They are both fine people, but they don't care about you.

No major gift happens without a relationship. Gifts to your organization will come from people who know you and care about you.

How does that happen?

You have to grow your own major donors. You have to begin and nurture relationships with people who have the capacity and either have, or could develop, the interest to support you in that way.

So it begs the question, where do major donors come from? Is there a store somewhere? We wish!

<u>Giving is at the intersection of two sets, capacity and interest.</u> We can't change the prospective donor's capacity; they either have it, or they don't.

Interest is the relationship they feel they have with you.

If a relationship doesn't already exist, how does it begin?

The beginning of a relationship is like the spark that starts the campfire. We try and try and then all of a sudden, there it is! A spark! Be careful! Be gentle with it.

Pay close attention to it, especially in the beginning, or that little spark won't grow into a flame! Puff, puff – gently! Don't overdo it, or the spark will go out. But soon that little flame is established and grows.

How does that spark happen?

My boss was just beginning his remarks to an alumni group. The venue was a little noisy and I knew he was going to cut it short. A couple appeared in the back, then disappeared, and then they came back again.

They were agitated because they were late. There was nowhere to park. I finally got Bill and Kathy seated. They heard none of the president's talk and didn't seem to care.

This is when our smile is permanently affixed to our face. I introduced our two guests to my boss and then Bill and Kathy struck up a conversation with two ladies at their table.

A half hour later, I pulled up a chair and sat down next to Bill. As luck would have it, it turned out the president of our alumni association was a very close friend of Bill's. We had something in common.

I saw Bill's shoulders relax. Smiles came more easily to him. I glanced at his wife. Kathy was happy that her husband was happy. She directed her attention to the other two ladies at the table.

Bill had been on the football team. I told him the one story I knew about his old coach. Bill looked at me and said, "You know what? Coach saved my life." And he meant it.

Next thing I knew, Bill was trying to tell me something else about Coach, but he was so overcome with emotion he couldn't speak.

Tears filled his eyes. Kathy noticed. So did the other two ladies.

Bill looked at me as he dabbed his eyes. I nodded. Bill knew I understood. I said,

"I've seen in the archives the letter Coach wrote to the parents when you guys made the team. He must have been quite a guy."

Bill could barely get the words out.

"He was."

Five minutes later we were still talking. We weren't strangers now. Our tone of voice with each other was less formal and more familiar.

I asked, "When are you and Kathy back in Chicago?"

Bill told me they'd be back in the summer.

"Okay, when you're back, you and I and Phil (the alumni president) have to grab lunch together. Hey, wait, better than that," I said, "we'll play some golf!"

Bill loved it. Huge smile. Huge smile from Kathy.

When we said goodbye that night, I did the same four things I did when I met them. I looked them both square in the eye, I smiled, I said their names and I gave them both a "business" handshake.

Add a handwritten note when I got back to the office, and that relationship was off to the races.

Grow your own. You can do it. You have to create the occasion (build the campfire) and watch for the spark. But you have to pay attention. You can't be looking up into the trees.

Watch for the spark. It will come.

Listening

I checked my watch. 12:15 p.m. We were to meet for lunch at noon. Was I being stood up? That's an occupational hazard of ours.

Standing in the lobby of his country club, I peered out the window to the circular drive. A minivan eased into one of the handicapped spots by the front walk. The door opened. He exited slowly, leaning a bit on his cane.

I stepped outside to greet him. "Harry," I smiled, "it's good to see you again!" He returned the smile and my extended hand.

This was our second meeting. The first was at his home. A great big house, it echoed with the emptiness of grown children gone from the nest and a spouse claimed by cancer a year ago.

At that first meeting Harry had a friend join us, a "wing man" of sorts. So when Harry called me, out of the blue, and asked me to join him for lunch at his club, I was gratified by the trust that seemed to be developing between us.

"Good afternoon Mr. Donahue!"

The dining room of every club has a sentry posted behind an enormous podium. This nice lady greeted Harry with affection.

"Marian, where are you putting us today?" he answered with a smile. We walked slowly through the tables to a quiet spot by the window. I offered my host a chair so his back would be to the sun streaming in.

I don't care how many visits you've made, the first question to start the meeting is always a cautious moment. This is the time when the other person is "reading" us. Are we nervous? Rushed?

25

Cocky? We usually aim for "quiet confidence" with the emphasis on "quiet."

My question about his weekend lead to another about his family then, "Can I ask, how did you meet your wife?" and somehow all this led to a story about Harry's early career.

It seems disjointed in the retelling, but at the moment it was exactly what it was supposed to be – a conversation. It was a conversation with the fundraiser doing most of the listening.

He answered my questions with relish, as if to say, "You know what, thank you for asking. Thank you for listening with sincerity. Thank you for letting me be heard."

I thought, "No, Harry, the thanks go to you. This is wonderful. Illuminating. Fun. Listening to you is helping me understand why philanthropy is important to you and how I might be able to suggest a gift to meet your needs, not just mine.

"I daresay if I was yammering at you instead of listening, there would be no possible way to understand what is important to you.

"But I understand now."

He'd brought along a ratty old manila folder. Papers were falling out of it. A Wall Street Journal article he insisted I read. A photograph of his late wife. Drafts of a letter he'd started to friends for a fund in her memory.

I put my hand on his forearm and smiled. "Harry, I have to ask you a question. Looking at Dorothy's picture, she seems to have been quite the catch. How did you manage that?"

His eyes immediately filled with tears and he answered through those tears. "We were married 57 years. She was the most beautiful girl I ever knew. I miss her so much."

We just sat there for a minute. Then Harry said, "You know, you and I are separated in age by a generation and yet I feel we have so much in common." I just nodded.

"Harry," I finally asked him, "If I put together some thoughts about how we could move this project forward, create a memorial to your wife and invite your children to get involved, would that be something you'd like to see?"

"Yes," he told me. "Yes, I would like that very much."

I never cease to be awed by the power of listening. When we first start out as fundraisers, we are less sure of ourselves and we may try to control the meeting by talking 90 percent of the time. Our epiphany comes when we realize the person who talks the least is the one who controls the conversation.

We build trust by listening. And we learn what is important to our donors.

To me, listening is the most difficult – and the most important – skill of our craft to master. Very few people do it well.

I'm still learning.

Mary

When I stepped off the elevator, I wasn't sure where her apartment door was.

"Over here!" I heard a slight voice call. She was standing in the doorway, her hands of 90-plus years gripping her walker.

"Mary, how are you?" I smiled and hustled over to her.

"What did you bring?" she demanded to know. She didn't miss a trick. I was trying to hide the little cake from the bakery under the book I was delivering to her.

"I know you said not to bring anything but I'm sorry, my mother taught me not to come empty-handed. It's just something for your dessert tonight. I think you'll like it," and I smiled hopefully.

"Oh, you have some Irish in you, don't you?"

She wasn't upset. She was pleased, actually. I followed Mary into her apartment. She made her way over to her chair by the window. Her reading lamp was close by, along with her glasses and other "accessories."

"I'm just going to put this in the kitchen for you," I called and then I hurried back in and showed Mary the book. The president had inscribed a short greeting to her on the inside front cover.

"My goodness, how nice!" She was touched. "Sit down now," and she pointed to another chair.

This wasn't a visit to ask. It was a visit to visit.

"It's great to see you!" I said, but I walked right into it.

"How long has it been?" Mary asked me, and I fibbed.

"Oh, I think six or eight months?" and she called me out.

"No, the last time you stopped by I was just back from rehab at the nursing home. That was 15 months ago."

She knew exactly. I felt terrible. I told her so, told her I was sorry, and all was forgiven.

When you are visiting an older person, you don't need to prepare much. An "ice breaker" or two (the cake and the book), and then you ask a question and you sit back and listen. It is why you are there. To listen.

That's the real gift you bring, so much more meaningful than a cake or a book. You are listening.

We talked about all sorts of things. An illness she was dealing with. Her brother's 88-year-old prostate. I sat there thinking, "What a privilege to have her confidence; heck, to be invited into her home!"

We told each other a joke or two. Her jokes were better than mine. We laughed, hard. We agreed that laughter is a good thing.

"I have four causes that mean the most to me," Mary told me, and I knew mine was one of them. She told me why they are meaningful to her.

And then it came. Out of the blue. Like a thunderbolt. How I wish you could have been there to hear it! I swear to you, she said exactly this:

"Do you know what really matters to me? This is the one thing that would make a person like me give more. When I hear from one of my causes what happens with my gift.

"When I hear about someone my gift is helping, that the person is trying, that they are succeeding, I tell you, I want to help them more!"

Mary told me about a student at one of her causes. She knew the young person's whole story! It was like talking with a 92-year-old development officer!

"Mary, that must make you feel good about your gift to them," I said.

"Feel good?" She looked at me as if I were dense. "It gives me a reason for living!"

It was time to go. I told Mary not to get up, but she did anyway. I leaned down and gave her a hug. She gave me a bigger hug back.

Six months later my phone rang. It was Mary's niece.

"I thought you should know," she said, "Mary is in home hospice. She doesn't have too much time left."

I asked if I could stop by, and I did. One last time. To say goodbye.

Mary was in bed, tucked under covers up to her chin. I've done some tough things in my life, but this was right up there at the top of the list.

"Well, isn't this a doozy," I stammered. What do you say?

"It sure is," my friend told me. "But I'm ready. You keep at it, now, promise me."

I told her I would. I bent down, kissed her cheek and whispered, "Thank you, Mary."

She squeezed my hand, smiled and said, "No, thank you."

Searching for those magic words to make a donor buckle at the knees will only disappoint you. Wait for that perfect moment to ask and you will only grow old.

It doesn't matter how you ask for a gift. Any words will do. What does matter is you've taken the time to listen. You know the donor has the ability to make the gift you seek. There's a relationship.

As with everything else in life, the more you do it, the easier it becomes and the better you are at it. Making visits and making the Ask are no different. Get out. Be your own good self. Your motivation is your sure knowledge of the good the gift will accomplish.

Just follow this path:

If you are behind your desk you are not raising money;

Personal visits are the key to building relationships;

You do not get what you do not ask for; and,

If you are not writing two thank you notes every morning, you are not doing your job.

The Third Truth:

Put the Donor First

It is not always about you.

The Prom

The development director was walking down the hall when a member of his team stopped him.

"Here, you should see this."

The flyer read:

Help Send the Students in Our Children's Program to Their Prom

Students in the Children's Program were profoundly disabled. The sheet explained the older students needed and deserved a prom at the end of the school year just like teens at other schools.

There were two columns on the page. To the left, the itemized costs for sending a boy to prom: the cost of tux rental, shoes, haircut, prom bid, et al. The total: $185.

On the right, the costs for a girl: hair, shoes, dress, flower, and prom bid: $215.

The flyer asked for help in sponsoring a student, or any of the individual costs.

The development director just stood there. He didn't know what to say. The dedication of these teachers to their students was overwhelming.

"What are they doing with this?" he asked his colleague.

"They don't know. There's a whole stack of 'em. I think they wanted us to see it. The teachers know we're in the middle of a campaign and didn't want to bother us, but there's no money to do this."

"Get 75 of the flyers. And please go tell the development officers that we're meeting at one o'clock in the conference room."

Within an hour, stamps, pens, monarch letterhead, and reply envelopes were rounded up. A list of lapsed, higher-end annual fund donors was quickly pulled. The development director cobbled together another list of names of donors who would be upset not to be included.

Included in what? His team was about to find out.

The six frontline fundraisers – major gifts, planned giving, annual fund and corporate/foundation relations – trooped into the conference room, with puzzled looks on their faces. A flyer about the prom was at each place.

The development director sat down, looked around the room and spoke to his team:

"Whatever you were going to do this afternoon," he said, "or at least for the next two or three hours, is going to have to wait. We all have a job to do right now that is much more important."

Everyone read the sheet. They nodded and smiled. This was more important.

Together, the fundraisers crafted a template letter on the whiteboard:

"Dear Mr. and Mrs. Jones,

We are writing you and a select group of friends today to invite your help in sending some wonderful young people to their prom..."

Knowing that the ultimate piece of direct mail is a handwritten letter with a handwritten envelope and a live stamp, each member of the team wrote ten personal letters, addressed ten envelopes, and stuffed each with their secret weapon, the flyer from the teachers in the Children's Program. Seventy-plus letters went out in the mail that afternoon.

The response? Astounding. Gifts poured in.

Many had notes enclosed with the check: "Thank you for giving us the opportunity to participate." "Our family wants to send both a boy and a girl to their prom." "I am honored to give." "We are so proud to be part of such a wonderful organization."

In five days, the money was raised to send every one of the older students to their prom.

The development team reconvened soon after in the conference room for their weekly staff meeting. There was a soft knock. It was the Director of the Children's Program. She was standing in the doorway, holding something, tears streaming down her face.

"I'm sorry to interrupt. My teachers don't know what to say to all of you. They baked this cake to thank you."

She looked around the room and struggled to get the words out. "You all have a very tough job. I don't know if you've ever felt like heroes. But right now, all of you are heroes to us."

She set the cake down, walked over to the Development Director, and hugged him.

Of course, the fundraisers invited the prom donors to attend the big event. It was held at a local hotel. Many came, some in tuxedos and formal dresses. The students grinned from ear to ear. Teachers, parents, donors and fundraisers were overcome with emotion all night.

A few weeks later, the development director was having a beer with an old friend and told him the story of the Prom.

"I can't figure it out," he said. "The gifts - it was such an outpouring. I don't know what triggered it all."

His wise friend looked at him. "Are you serious? I don't know much about your business, but the story you just told me? That's what fundraising should be all about all the time.

"Let me be honest," he continued, "people really don't care about your annual funds or your capital campaigns. Those are artificial constructions that your business creates.

"Those donors? They wanted to do one thing. They wanted to send a kid to the prom. Period. That's what you asked them to do, and that's what people want to hear. When we give, we want to know that our gift will make a difference. Your job is to show us how."

That's impact philanthropy in a nutshell. When we extend an invitation to our donors to invest in us, we need to remember for whom, for what, and why.

We need to remember the prom.

Jane Newman's Journey

It was the Tuesday before Thanksgiving and the office was starting to clear out for the holiday. She answered the phone on the second ring.

"Hello, Jane Newman."

"Jane, this is Carl Stevenson."

She sat bolt upright and began to panic. There was always something wrong when Carl called. She forced a smile.

"Carl, how good to hear your voice! Happy Thanksgiving!"

"Yeah, okay, listen. Marge and I would like to see you. Can you come down here?" It didn't sound like a request, more like an order.

"Of course! I'd love to! What day next week works best for you?"

"No, not next week. Now. Tomorrow. We have something on our mind we want to tell you."

"Oh, absolutely then. You bet. I'm sure I can make it there tomorrow. (She lied.) Would around lunchtime be okay?"

"Yeah, that's fine. Wait - what? O, Marge says hello. Okay then, we'll see you here tomorrow." Click.

Jane sat still for a second, looking at the telephone. What just happened? Marge Stevenson was a dear lady, but Carl was a world-class pain in the you-know-where. Their annual checks to the organization were just large enough to demand his persnickety nature be tolerated.

As she started looking for a flight leaving and returning on the day before Thanksgiving, Jane knew it was hopeless. Ten minutes of clicking confirmed her suspicions. She took a deep breath, packed up her briefcase, and drove home.

"You're going WHERE?" Her husband was lounging with a beer and the newspaper.

"Jack, please don't start. I have to drive to Hilton Head Island to meet with the Stevensons. They just called and want to see me tomorrow, and there are no flights."

"Jane, I know it's your job, but really? It's Thanksgiving!"

"You just answered your own question," she replied. "This is my job. It's a 9-hour drive. I'll stay somewhere tonight, head back tomorrow afternoon and I'll be home by noon on Thanksgiving. We'll be on time for dinner at your folks'."

Jane went upstairs, packed an overnight bag, kissed her husband, and headed out.

Truth be told, she didn't really mind these long drives. Jane found the "peace and quiet" to be soothing, and there was time to sort out the tenuous balance of work and family. She sipped on a bottle of water, grabbed a burger somewhere and after a long day, found a Hampton Inn for the night.

She was back on the road by 7 a.m. Coffee replaced the bottle of water in her Camry. As Hilton Head drew near Jane started to fret. What went wrong? What did she do? Racking her brain, she came up with nothing. By the time she pulled into the

Stevenson's circular driveway a little after noon, Jane was a tired mess.

"This is not going to beat me," she decided. "Whatever they want, we'll figure it out. I'm proud of myself that I'm here."

The enormous front door opened quickly and there was Carl; 75 or so, over 6 feet tall and way over 200 pounds. The little construction company he founded 47 years ago had grown by leaps and bounds. Carl Stevenson still looked like he could frame a house by himself.

"Well, hello there! You made it! Thanks for stopping down on such short notice. Your flight was okay?"

He was smiling. This was new.

"Hi, well, actually, I drove." She tried her best to return the smile.

"You what?"

"I tried, but there weren't any flights I could grab. You know, the holiday and all. No worries, I'm glad to see you!"

Just then Marge walked into the foyer. Carl turned to her. "Marge, she drove here."

The kind lady was shaken. "Oh, Jane, we are so embarrassed! My goodness, you must be exhausted! Come in, do you need to use the restroom? Let me get you some iced tea!"

Marge whirled around in three directions and Carl stood there looking sheepish. They finally adjourned to the living room and settled in.

To Jane's surprise, Marge spoke first. In all her experience with them, Carl always ran the show. But, somehow, today was different.

"My dear, we are so sorry you had to make such a long trip. But we want to tell you something and it just couldn't wait. We've made a decision and it involves you. Carl, go ahead."

"Jane," he started, "it's like this." Carl was fumbling for words. This was really different. "We – okay, I – have been really crabby to you for a long time."

Jane tried to politely disagree, but Carl waved her off.

"No, thank you, you're being polite, but the truth is, I've been a real pill. And all these years, you've stayed the course. You kept in touch, kept us up to date on things and you never gave up on us, even when we played really hard-to-get. We respected you for that. We never told you so, but we did, and we do."

Jane tried her best not to look stunned. She'd heard about this before, how relationships can turn on a dime, but she had never experienced it. She had nothing to say. But then, Carl and Marge weren't looking for her to say anything. They had a lot more to tell their guest.

"Our grandson just came back from one of your service trips," Carl continued. "We don't know what was in the water down there, but we hear he came back a changed person. Marge and I thought we should do a little something to thank you all, and then it happened.

"The more we thought about making a gift, the happier we got."

Now it was Marge's turn. "Jane, when you get to be old like us – don't shake your head, yes, we're old – you think about two

41

things. All the time. They're pretty much the only two things you think about.

"Seniors like us think about losing control. We lose our health, our memories a little bit, our friends, our ability to drive, all sorts of things.

"And we think about our legacy. Who's going to remember us when we're gone. Oh, sure, our family, but who else?"

"And then we 'got it.' Making a gift to you wonderful people fixed both of those things. We felt we were back in charge again. It was wonderful! And we thought, maybe we could do something with our name on it, and people might remember us, that we tried to help."

The most amazing thing happened. Carl Stevenson wiped a tear from his cheek.

"Listen to me now." His voice was gentle, but firm. "Our kids and grandkids are coming down tomorrow and we're telling them what we plan to do. We can't wait. We are thankful that finally, after all these years, we figured this out. Here."

He reached in his pocket, pulled out a letter and with a shaking hand, passed it to Jane. It was addressed to the president, Jane's boss, informing her that $3 million in stock had been transferred that morning to the organization's account.

Carl grinned. "Bet you thought we forgot those stock transfer instructions you sent us way back when, didn't you?! Well, we didn't!" He was like an excited kid.

For Jane, this was one of those moments that define a career. Shaking her head in wonderment she took Carl's hand in hers, mouthed her thanks, and turned to embrace Marge.

As they hugged, Jane thanked her.

"No, dear," was Marge's whispered reply. "I thank you. Thank you for giving us our grandson back."

And with a last squeeze she whispered, "And thank you for giving me my husband back."

"Okay, now, you scoot!" Carl was back in charge, trying to calm the emotion in the room. "You have a family to get back to for Thanksgiving, I imagine. You'll make it in time? You have a place to stay tonight?"

Now he was the one making the fuss. Marge quickly packed up sandwiches for Jane's long drive home.

One last round of hugs, and one last "thank you" from a grateful development officer. They waved from the doorway.

Jack threw open the front door when he heard the car. "You made it! Everything go okay?"

"They made a really big gift," Jane sighed. "But that wasn't the best part."

"What was the best part, then?"

"I'll tell you later. It's complicated. I'm really tired now."

"Okay, but I need to tell you something."

"What's that?"

"I'm so proud of you."

"Why won't they make a gift?" We hear that so often, we think it's the Great Central Mystery of fundraising.

It's not. The Great Mystery is why we consistently refuse to put the donor first.

"Hey, tell me how this looks to you." We corral a colleague about a letter or a donor strategy. Why aren't we asking instead, "Tell me how you think this will look to our donor."

We spend so much time focusing on OUR objectives for the visit, what WE want to accomplish with the letter, that we sail right past how it will appear to the person who receives it.

We spend an enormous amount of time thinking about how to form a relationship with a donor. Let's take just a minute to ask, "I wonder who the donor feels they have a relationship with here?"

The single best piece of advice I received in my entire career was when a young colleague had the nerve and the courage to remind me, "Rob, it's not always about you."

The Golden Rule of Fundraising: Do unto the donor as you would do unto yours.

The Fourth Truth:

Say Thank You

It is more important to be great
at saying thank you for the gift
than it is to be great at asking for the gift.

The Campaign

"Well, they're waiting for me," I thought. "Here we go."

The development team was gathered in the conference room for our monthly staff meeting. Twelve pairs of eyes stared at me as I sat down at the end of the long table.

Each face wore a look of nervous anticipation. That day, at that meeting, we would begin the campaign, a $20 million effort to coincide with the organization's centennial. It would be by far the largest fundraising effort in our history.

This was a team of talented, but new, advancement professionals. Without saying a word, they were all asking me the same question:

"Are you sure we can do this?"

I looked at each person and asked my own question. "So, here we are, about to begin the biggest challenge we'll ever face together. What makes us think we even have a chance? There are hundreds of worthy organizations in town, all fighting for our donors and their philanthropy.

"What makes us think for a minute we can compete against the museum? The medical center? Or the university, for goodness sake! Are we nuts?

"It seems to me for us to have a chance to compete, to make our campaign goal, we have to be better at something than everyone else. We have to find that one thing that will allow us to be David against these many Goliaths.

"I've decided what that one thing is going to be. For every day of the campaign, we are going to be better than everyone else at saying 'thank you.' Together, we are going to commit to making every one of our donors feel truly appreciated for their gift."

Saying thank you in the most genuine way possible became our mantra. Every donor of $200 or more received a phone call from a member of the team. A lot of campaign visits resulted from those calls! Every gift received a hand-signed letter of thanks. Recognition of the larger gifts got the same strategic approach as the solicitation of that gift.

As the months passed and the campaign inched ahead, we began to realize we were on to something.

Fast forward 18 months. Concurrent with the campaign, a key element of the anniversary celebration was presenting centennial medals to donors and friends who had advanced the work of the organization in a significant way.

On this particular morning a few of us were in the 20th floor office of the chairman and CEO of one of the city's largest and most respected companies.

Ted and Sally as a couple, as well as the company itself, were true friends of the organization and it was an honor to recognize them. Our president made the presentation of the medal to Ted. Sally, a member of our board looked on proudly as did Bill, the company's director of community relations.

After the presentation and photos, smiles and handshakes were exchanged all around. Bill spoke up.

"Ted, would you mind if I said something?"

This was not in the script. The CEO looked a little tentative but, ever the gentleman said, "Of course, Bill."

And Bill turned to face us.

"You folks know our company works with a lot of nonprofits."

We nodded to this understatement.

"And we give away a lot of money every year."

We nodded again.

"I need to tell you sincerely that you do a better job of saying 'thank you' than anyone else in town."

There it was. Mission accomplished. Ted and Sally nodded in agreement. We thanked Bill for a compliment that meant more to us than he would ever know.

By the way, we completed the campaign. On time and on goal. To this day, I am convinced that making donors feel truly appreciated is what it takes to win.

Disappointment

I was having coffee with a friend of mine. She's the director of development for a wonderful nonprofit. Among other things we were talking about our year-end totals and all the thank-you letters those gifts precipitate.

My friend had a sad look on her face. I asked if anything was the matter.

"No, sorry. We had a really great year end. Very fortunate. A lot of hard work by our team. I just had a personal experience with a thank you that wasn't so great."

I asked, if it wasn't prying, would she tell me?

"Sure. Actually, I've been wishing I could share it with someone, but my family and personal friends wouldn't understand.

"You know where I went to college, right? It was a wonderful time of my life. When I started in development, I had grandiose ideas of being a big donor to my alma mater. I owe them a lot.

"But life got in the way." She smiled. "Now I sound like one of my own donors!"

"My husband and I put our kids through private school, and you know where they went to college. It was really hard for us to make that work but we did. In the meantime, my giving to my own college was nowhere near where I wanted it to be. It was sporadic and not up to my intentions. I was embarrassed about it, but we had responsibilities.

"Anyway, last December I told my husband I wanted to get serious about giving to them on a regular basis. We talked about starting at a modest level and increasing our gift every year, then including my college in our estate plan later on. We talked about them a lot, and a couple other causes we wanted to ramp up our giving to.

"So I sent my school $250. I know it's not a world-beater, but to be honest, I was really excited to write that check. I even called someone in their development office to watch out for my gift because I didn't have an envelope from them. I guess I was reliving what I had always wanted my giving to my college to be and now I was going to make it happen.

"It made me happy."

I took a sip of coffee and told my friend, "Well, so far so good!"

"You're right. Now, don't laugh. I started watching the mail for my thank-you letter. I was like a little kid. It finally came one day."

"By the look on your face, it wasn't what you hoped for."

"Oh, the letter was fine, I guess. It said all the correct things. But it was a form letter. The signer was the vice president. His signature was imprinted at the bottom.

"It was a lousy imprint.

"There's no way that VP ever got within 25 feet of that letter, or my gift. It was so obvious it was prepared by someone in their development operations office.

"You know what? I really wish that person had signed my letter instead."

I told my friend I felt badly for her experience. Was this going to affect her future giving to her college?

"To be honest, I don't know. I'm still sorting out how I feel. It was probably my own fault for getting my hopes up. I don't know what I expected.

"It was only $250.

"Deep down, I don't feel I was thanked for my gift.

"I feel like I was processed."

Your Competitive Edge

There is something your competition hopes you never learn. Especially the big organizations that look so invincible.

"Oh, we could never compete with them for that donor's affections!"

Well, yes you can, if you know this secret. To compete, to succeed, you have to be better at one thing than any other organization your donors support. You have to be the best, the very best, at saying thank you.

Other organizations, especially those bigger than you, really hope you don't figure this out. Because the one silver bullet you have in your holster is that you can be better at thanking your donors than any organization they support.

You just have to choose to be. And if you do, you can compete with anybody. Can you make your $1,000 donor feel more appreciated for their gift than the big university can? Yes indeed. Actually, that's easy to do.

There is one thing you can do with your $1,000 donor that the big nonprofit cannot do. You can be more immediate, more personal, and more impactful to that donor in the way you say thank you.

It's simple math. The big nonprofit receives many more $1,000 gifts than you do. So many that the way they express their thanks for that gift is far less personal than you can be! You know it, I know it, and trust me, they know it.

They just hope you won't do anything about it because if you choose to, you can be more successful in thanking that donor than the big nonprofit.

A friend told me, "My spouse and I made a $1,000 gift to a big university. We were so disappointed by the impersonal way we were thanked. A few days later we received an email from one of the program staff. We had made our gift in his name. Here's what he wrote:

'I just wanted to thank you for the unbelievably kind donation in my name. It was totally out of the blue and just one of those random acts of kindness that makes you want to pass it along. We have lots of exciting things in the hopper for the coming year. We couldn't do it without people like you. Sincerely, thank you so much.'"

My friend told me, "We will make another gift to that organization next year, solely because of that note.

It made us feel appreciated. Their development office did not."

There are three things we know about human nature. People need to be wanted. To know they can make a difference. And people need to feel appreciated. They desperately need to feel appreciated and they rarely do.

Whoever you are, wherever you work, big shop or little shop, if you can say thank you better than your competition, you will win.

The Note

I was giving a tour to Jim and Mary McAdams. Jim was an alumnus of the school and president of a huge company based in Florida. They were in town visiting family and Mary had never seen her husband's alma mater.

The timing was perfect. Jim's reunion was coming up in a few months and I wanted them to consider a reunion gift. All the pieces were in place.

The McAdams were terribly nice people and we quickly developed a nice connection. When we sat down in my office, I didn't waste much time and asked them to consider a gift of $25,000 to renovate and name a computer classroom.

They gulped.

I thought fast. "Jim and Mary, if it helps, you could make your gift with stock. You'll get a tax deduction on the full present value of your gift and at the same time avoid the capital gains tax on the appreciated value of the stock."

Mary looked at her husband and said, "You know, Jim, we could do that." And they did.

Reunion Weekend began on a crystal-clear autumn Friday. The school and its alumni director were about to welcome four classes that night and there was a big list of last-minute tasks.

At the top of my list was Jim McAdams. In the months since he and Mary made their gift, the computer classroom had been completed. Twenty-four sparkling new computer stations were installed, and the original wood floor had been stripped and polished until it shone. A rather large plaque hung on the wall outside the classroom announcing it to the world The McAdams Computer Resource Lab.

I needed Jim to see the room.

It was almost not to be. At 11 in the morning I began to get phone calls from Jim's assistant.

"He's been called into a meeting with the Chairman and has to catch a later flight."

"Well, that flight left without him. I'm going to try to get him on a flight that will land about 4:30."

I stressed about it the whole day. Jim rarely got to Chicago and a big part of our thanks to him and Mary was to show him the lab. As each hour passed, I felt the chances of that happening were slipping away.

In the middle of reunion details, I stopped by the classroom to see the teacher, Barb. I asked if she could stick around for just a little bit after school to meet our benefactor and give him a tour of the lab he'd funded. Gracious as always, Barb agreed.

Finally, when it was clear Jim wasn't going to arrive until after 6 p.m., Barb told me she had to leave.

"But I wrote him a note on the blackboard. If you go in the room, you'll see it."

At last, Jim McAdams arrived at his reunion. I saw him in the crowd checking in at the registration table. He was roaring with laughter with his classmates. I could tell by the look on his face, the poor guy just wanted to get a cold beer and visit with his pals.

I was having none of that.

I gently tugged at his sleeve. "Jim, can I steal you for a moment? I really want you to see the computer lab you and Mary funded. Could we?"

It was the last thing Jim wanted to do but, ever the gentleman, off we went. As we got close to the classroom door, I grandly gestured to the bronze plaque. It might as well have been a fly on the wall. It made no impression on him whatsoever.

I started to sweat. I opened the door of the room, clicked on the lights and we both turned to the right to see the computer workstations. Now, I saw a hint of approval on his face. But he still wanted to get back downstairs.

"Jim, I asked the teacher if she could stay to say hello to you. She had to leave, but she left you a note."

We turned around and on the blackboard we read:

"Mr. McAdams, this lab means so much to our students. For them, I thank you from the bottom of my heart. Enjoy your reunion!"

And she signed her name at the bottom.

Jim stared at the blackboard without saying a word. This titan of industry had tears welling in his eyes. I started to tear up myself. Here were two grown men who barely knew one another, standing alone in a deserted classroom, trying hard to keep our composure.

I had to say something.

"Jim, Barb really wanted to thank you herself. She hoped this note would tell you how much she, and all of us, appreciate the gift you and Mary have made."

After a moment he turned away from the blackboard, looked at me and said in a quiet, steady voice, "Well, you just tell her, this won't be the last."

And I assure you, it wasn't.

Show the impact of the gift. Say thank you. Every time.

I was asked once, "What's the worst mistake a fundraiser can make?"

As I sat and thought, really thought, about those things that can sink a fundraiser, I realized that most everything comes down to one simple thing:

Never make a donor feel small.

Every donor matters. He or she would like to think they matter to you and your organization. If we as fundraisers ever give the donor the clear impression, whether from a form acknowledgment letter, not returning a call, cutting a visit short or whatever, that they don't matter to us, you can kiss their support and that relationship goodbye.

In any relationship, the other person wants to know they matter to you.

Winning

The Fifth Truth:

Focus on the Right Things

It gets discouraging to see fundraisers all over the country spending so much time focusing on the wrong things. We fret about things that, to the donor, really don't matter. We spend way too much effort thinking about HOW donors will make their gift instead of helping them know WHY they should care about our cause. How donors make their gift is going to change. It has over the years and will in the future. Why that person, that couple, that family decide to support you, those motivations have remained the same for a hundred years, and always will.

Dreading Sunday Night

It's Sunday night. The dinner dishes have been put away. Maybe you've finished that second glass of wine. You find your bag or briefcase and set it on the kitchen counter for the morning, wondering what you'll toss in there for lunch tomorrow.

Your mind wanders to the week ahead. What are you thinking?

Does the work week fill you with anticipation? Or unease?

Do you dread Sunday night?

That's not good. There's a big difference between taking a deep breath knowing you have a busy week ahead, and secretly wishing you would come down with the flu so you could stay home.

Deep down, what you wish you were thinking is:

"Buckle up!" "I'm going to kick some tail and take no prisoners!" "Not sure what, but I'm gonna make something happen this week!"

That feeling of positive anticipation? The best way I've ever heard it expressed is "I want to 'bring it' every day."

Moving from a feeling of dread to "Let's go!" takes addressing one or more of five things that stand in your way.

If you think of the week ahead as one big 500-pound bear, you will lose. You can't dance with a bear. You have to break up the week into smaller, manageable pieces you can attack and conquer one at a time.

Two, admit to yourself you aren't going to convert Mother Russia next week. As you lay out your week in your mind, or in your planner, be kind to yourself and set realistic goals you can actually achieve. The rest can wait. Really, it can wait. For once, give yourself permission to succeed this week.

Among the goals that you do embrace for your week have to be the three most important to-do's on your list. You know what those are. The task we most want to avoid? We convince ourselves it can wait a little longer. Stop avoiding. Most often the task we dislike the most is the most important. Know the top three things you need to get done next week and commit to them.

Part of the reason you have that knot in your stomach is because your boss doesn't know what you have on your plate, or because you and your boss aren't on the same page when it comes to your priorities. You have to fix that.

Believe me when I tell you, if your boss wants to know what you are doing, the two of you need to be on the same page. She or he has to know your priorities and agree with them. If that doesn't happen, no matter what else you do, that knot in your stomach isn't going to go away.

Finally, you have to close the door. Literally or figuratively. If you know your priorities, if your boss does, if they're realistic, and if they're in manageable bites, that is your focus for the week. You really don't care how busy everyone else is. Saying to a colleague, "Sure, I can help you with that" becomes a very low priority.

Because the truth is, no one cares how busy you are.

That sounds unbelievable harsh, I know, but it's true. Not even your closest friend in the office cares how busy you are. He or she has their own work to do and you have yours. Keep it that way.

Please, don't get me wrong. Being a team player is very important to me as a colleague and a boss. But one of the most profound pieces of professional advice I ever received was,

"Stop being such a nice guy."

In this case let's translate that to "Love others AS YOU LOVE YOURSELF."

Spending all your time looking after others and not looking after yourself is one of the five reasons you feel out of control, and one of the five reasons you dread Sunday night.

Let's change that.

The Rule

Over the years it has been my good fortune to know stellar fundraising professionals at many of the top development programs in the country. I have come to realize they share two traits in common.

One, they are all unfailingly nice people. While I suppose being nice contributes to their success, I nonetheless marvel at how such busy people always make time to share and encourage while having workloads and schedules that make me shudder.

The second trait? It is never written about in our literature and is rarely, if ever, a topic at conferences.

There are lots of nice people in development shops all across our country but the winners, those who truly raise the bar, they understand and practice one thing.

I call it "The Rule."

True winners understand their job. They bring a laser-like focus to the task at hand. And they never, ever allow anything to distract them from that task.

It is my considerable good fortune to count Dan Reagan as a friend. Dan served the University of Notre Dame for more than 20 years and managed two campaigns of more than $1 billion each.

I think of him as the Babe Ruth of fundraising. I asked Dan once to tell me why their fundraising was so successful, and he told me something profound.

"Rob, we know that every fundraiser, at shops large and small, deals with 'speed bumps' that get in the way of they work they need to do. The work they want to do and the work they were brought there to do.

"We all want to succeed. We all want to serve our institutions in the best way we can. We know that means getting out, developing and sustaining relationships, and inviting the investment.

"But the speed bumps are there, and too often they become roadblocks.

"Sadly, and too often, we put them there ourselves. Finding a good reason not to make that call to the donor, for example. And there can always be a 'good reason.'

"I think the culprit most often is the manager or the development leader or the CEO of the organization who puts those speed bumps, those roadblocks, in our path.

"When we look at successful programs, and I include ours among them, there are no speed bumps or roadblocks.

"We remove them. We are intentional about removing them. We are relentless about removing them.

"Nothing gets in the way of the development officer doing the work he or she is there to do.

"I know that's easier at bigger shops with more hands on deck. But it comes down to a decision each of us has to make, every day.

"If we want to win, if we want to make our visits and our asks, we must remove those speed bumps."

How many distractions do you deal with every day? It can be overwhelming and often discouraging. We lament, "If I didn't have to deal with all of this, imagine what I could get done!"

Those who know The Rule understand those distractions never go away. They have mastered the art of not permitting myriad distractions from diverting them from the work they know will bring real impact.

It is astonishing to see the top achievers in our profession serve their institutions in the highest form by understanding The Rule and using it to their benefit every day.

Like I said, this is never discussed, but it is known. For a long time, I thought it was just my own take in things, but as you meet and get to know the highest achievers in our field, they shout The Rule out loud in how they approach their work every day.

Claudia Looney was for years one of America's foremost fundraisers. Author, speaker, chief development officer, and recipient of the Association of Fundraising Professionals highest honor.

In a profile in the AFP Magazine, Claudia was asked what, in her opinion, was the secret to fundraising success.

"To me, the answer to achieving our highest calling lies in knowing what NOT to do. Each of us faces so many demands on our time every day that pull us away from real success.

"Having the discipline to focus on those things that really matter, to me that is the most important thing."

Remove the roadblocks. Learn what not to do.

That is The Rule, and the road to winning.

If we need any further encouragement of the need to focus on the right things, we can look no further than the runaway success of the book "Donor-Centered Fundraising" by Penelope Burk.

Think about it for a minute. If the idea of putting the donor's needs and wants ahead of our own was so revolutionary to so many, do you suppose we've been focused for too long on the wrong priorities?

Focus on the right things.

Epilogue:

This Noble Work

Think about the millions of people in our country who volunteer at a nonprofit organization. They say to themselves and to others, "My life is more complete, and I feel more fulfilled by giving my time and effort to a cause I believe in."

Fundraisers get paid to do the same thing, every day.

We are the lucky ones.

Tilting at Windmills

Helen looked around the university's Phonathon Center. It was in the basement of the administration building; tucked away, but spacious enough for their needs. Campus security was great about stopping by and making them feel safe, even late in the evening when the rest of the building was deserted.

There were 20 caller cubicles but only 11 were staffed tonight, the Tuesday before the holiday. Many of Helen's student callers were already heading home. She was the Phonathon Director. It was a killer job that no one did for more than two or three years. The hours were just too tough. Helen hoped her dedication would be a stepping-stone to a "normal" development job in Alumni House across the Quad.

It was almost 10 p.m. Helen knew her team would be wrapping up their West Coast calls and sure enough, one by one, bleary-eyed students trooped up to her desk to deposit the evening's paperwork. Helen would do the report in the morning and head to the airport herself.

She loved how the students chatted amongst themselves at the end of their shift. Who had the biggest gift, who had the most hang-ups. They didn't take those personally. No good fundraiser takes the "no's" personally, she always reminded them.

Tonight, the chatter was about going out for a beer. "Beth, are you coming?"

Beth was a senior and the best caller by far. She had a wonderful phone manner you just can't teach, she had persistence, and she needed the money her 12 hours a week earned her.

"No thanks, you guys go ahead. Have a great holiday!"

68

As Beth called out over the top of her cubicle, Helen noticed that Beth's smile was forced.

"You ready to head out?"

Helen had wrapped up for the night. Beth was still sitting at her workstation.

"I guess so."

But she didn't move.

Almost by instinct Helen pulled a chair up close to Beth's and in a gentle but firm voice said, "Tell me what's wrong."

That was all it took. The floodgates opened. Tears streamed down Beth's cheeks. She was sobbing. Beth was sobbing so hard she was shaking.

"I don't know. It's silly."

She had to make an effort just to get the words out. Helen sat there, a foot away, stunned.

"Well, I'm here. It's just us. Tell me."

"Helen, I know this is stupid of me, but I am so scared! I mean, everything happening in our country and around the world these days! It's craziness! I think about if I would ever get married some day and want children, but who in their right mind would want to bring children into a world like ours! Really! Where are we going!

"And this! (Beth made a sweeping motion with her arm around the room.) I mean, I'm not trying to be disrespectful, but what good is all this?

"What difference does it make? In the big picture, I mean? Do you ever think about it? Fundraising just seems so inconsequential to me right now."

She reached out to Helen and touched her forearm.

"Helen, I'm so sorry. I didn't mean it to come out like that. I know you want this to be your career. I think you are an amazing person. I mean, I guess I really just don't know any more."

Sometimes the moment in front of us calls us to be a greater person than who we think we are.

Helen reacted not with anger or disdain to the young woman still weeping next to her. She sat forward on her chair, clasped her hands in her lap, and reached out from her heart to the frightened woman eight inches away.

"Hey, listen. Can you look at me for a second?"

Beth was trying to avert her eyes but looked across through her tears to Helen.

"I'm just as nervous about all of this as you are. Everybody I know is shaken. We don't know what's next. Things we thought we could count on, we're not sure anymore. But then I think about my life, what we take for granted and I realize how lucky we are. How thankful we should be, about so much.

"I know what you mean about calling. It's hard, night after night. But the amazing thing about life is we never know. We never know if someone you connect with might just be inspired to do something astounding. Here, or even someplace else. A kid whose scholarship is renewed because we raised the money for it? What do we know? That kid might someday figure out all the craziness in the world.

"You're right about this career I want to have, you know!"

By now the sobs had stopped, tissues were out, and a panicked face was now a hopeful face. Helen continued.

"I had lunch last week with Connie. Do you know her? She's amazing. She's been doing major gifts here forever. What a lady. I could never be like her, but I'm going to try!" Helen grinned.

"Connie told me that if you ask any fundraiser; that is, if you could get them to tell you the truth, they would tell you they're in this business for two reasons.

"First is, there will always be a need for people to do this work. If you can learn, if you're any good at it, you'll pretty much always be able to find a job. The pay's not Silicon Valley, but it's not flipping burgers, either.

"And the second is, she told me, every fundraiser has a little Don Quixote in them. Maybe we're tilting at windmills, maybe not.

"But every fundraiser hopes, and believes, that he or she can make the world a better place. Even a little bit. Even if it's just in their little corner of the world.

"That's what Connie told me. And you know what? I'm in. I want that. If I have to work, that's what I want my work to be about.

"If I really believe that fundraisers can at least try to make the world a better place, when all this craziness is going on, you better believe we're not going to stop trying.

"And neither, my friend, are you."

Helen stood up. Beth stood up. There was a hug that neither of them would soon forget.

Helen said, "Come on. Did I hear something about a beer?"

Reaching for the Stars

A few years ago, I had the opportunity to meet a fellow named John. He was the development director for a nonprofit organization in our nation's heartland.

John came over to development from the program side and was giving it everything he had. Even in the short time we had together I could tell he wanted so badly to succeed; not for himself so much, but because he believed to his bones in the work of his organization.

But he was unsure. I could see it in his eyes. "Am I on the right path? Is this going to work?" I wanted to put my arm around his shoulder to reassure him.

After a half day together, I needed to catch a plane. John and I never met again. I think of him, wishing we had one last afternoon together.

Here's what I would tell him:

"John, my friend, you are my hero. You do this work because you believe your organization makes the world a better place.

"You feel you are 'winging it' much of the time and it's a scary feeling for you. Don't be afraid. Especially, never be afraid to win. Far too many people in our business are afraid to win.

"Pay attention to the lessons you have learned and to the people who taught them to you. If one or two of the stories I've shared can guide you, then I am very glad.

"Believe in yourself. You know far more about fundraising than you think you do. So much of our work, after all, is plain old common sense.

"We really are the lucky ones. Every day we witness the best of human nature, the desire by our fellow human beings to help someone else. We see how their giving transforms our organizations and the lives of people there.

"We cherish victories big and small we struggled to achieve. We shoulder the setbacks and try to do better next time. Mostly, we work at this craft because we get to see the joy of philanthropy.

"Not many other people experience joy in their work.

"Never forget what our donors want from us. They want goodness.

"There is far too much crummy stuff in our world today. But you and your organization, to your donors you represent goodness. You represent hope there can be more good than bad in our world.

"You are reaching for the stars and taking your donors with you.

"Never forget that. You are a winner in my eyes."

Acknowledgments

This book was a long time coming. So many friends and colleagues were steadfast in their encouragement.

Jon Heintzelman kept nudging every so often asking, "How's the book coming?" Dan Reagan did the same. I am grateful to them.

Joe Hallissey told me, "Just focus on the writing" and he shepherded everything else. I am in awe of his expertise and owe him my profound thanks. Christa Rooks had the unenviable task of editing the book and made it better.

Joan Klaus is a visionary in the truest sense. She helped me see the path from a random collection of stories into the proper structure of a book. At the eleventh hour I was really stuck, and Brooke Voss offered a suggestion that made a huge difference. It was the kindness of Deb Flores in sending me a quote that got me off my duff and helped me finish.

Marilyn Benuska is an incredible fundraiser and friend. So many times I have benefited from her wise counsel.

Thanks to the Hadley Institute, especially Brad Spinsby and Kat Equina, for their help in producing the audiobook. Ray Coughlan, Aliya Pitts and Megan Davison are exceptional professionals I am privileged to know. And Clyde Watkins has impacted the careers of countless fundraisers, including yours truly.

About the Author

For more than four decades, Rob Cummings has served as a development leader for many of the Chicago area's oldest and best-known institutions.

Through his deep understanding of the field, his enthusiasm and capacity to nurture the growth and commitment of development professionals, Rob has established a distinguished record of success in major gift solicitation and building strong development teams.

He personally managed three successful capital campaigns and has raised multiple seven-figure gifts. With clients throughout the Midwest, his consulting practice specializes in capital campaigns, coaching major gift fundraisers and growing sustainable development programs.

Rob is a regular teacher and presenter for AFP and other local and national organizations. He is the author of The *Weekend Briefing*, a weekly email combining development best practice with an inspiring message that resonates with senior professionals and new fundraisers alike.

He can be reached at rcummings@theweekendbriefing.com.

About
The Weekend Briefing

"Every week when I finish reading the Briefing I say to myself, 'You can do this.'" Mission accomplished.

The *Weekend Briefing* began on Sunday night, September 15, 2008, in the heart of the Great Recession. Lehman Brothers collapsed the next day. It was not the best of times to be a fundraiser.

That first Briefing was emailed to 19 development directors, all of whom worked without the resources many other shops take for granted.

Today, the *Weekend Briefing* is received every Sunday night by 1,500 advancement professionals in 41 states, Canada, Great Britain, and Australia. A reader wrote, "You talk about what all of us face every day. Sometimes I marvel how you know exactly what I am dealing with and what I need to hear."

You can subscribe to the *Weekend Briefing* at https://theweekendbriefing.com.